A Catechism Primer Copybook

Published By:

Catholic Homestead

strengthening your Catholic home
www.catholichomestead.org

Copyright 2016- Catholic Homestead
Darby, Montana

The typography of this book is the property of Catholic Homestead and may not be reproduced without written permission from the publisher

ISBN-13: 978-1530841394

ISBN-10: 1530841399

Name:_____

Year:_____

A Catechism Primer

of

Christian Doctrine

By Roderick MacEachen, D.D.

The Catholic University of America

Nihil obstat:

P.A. URIQUE, S.S., D.D.,
Censor deputatus

Imprimatur:

J. CARD. GIBBONS, *Archbishop of Baltimore*

Baltimore, November 2, 1910

PRAYERS

The Lord's Prayer

Our Father, who art in heaven, hallowed be Thy name; Thy kingdom come; Thy will be done on earth as it is in heaven. Give us this day our daily bread, and forgive us our trespasses as we forgive those who trespass against us; and lead us not into temptation, but deliver us from evil. Amen

The Angelic Salutation.

Hail Mary, full of grace! the Lord is with thee: blessed art thou amongst women, and blessed is the fruit of thy womb, Jesus. Holy Mary, Mother of God, pray for us sinners, now and at the hour of our death. Amen.

The Apostles' Creed

I believe in God, the Father Almighty,
Creator of heaven and earth; and in
Jesus Christ, His only Son, our Lord,
who was conceived by the Holy Ghost,
born of the Virgin Mary, suffered
under Pontius Pilate, was crucified,
died, and was buried. He descended into
hell; the third day He arose again from
the dead. He ascended into heaven,
sitteth at the right hand of God, the
Father Almighty; from thence He shall
come to judge the living and the dead. I

believe in the Holy Ghost, the Holy Catholic Church, the communion of Saints, the forgiveness of sins, the resurrection of the body, and the life everlasting. Amen.

The Confiteor

I confess to almighty God, to blessed Mary, ever Virgin, to blessed Michael the Archangel, to blessed John the Baptist, to the Holy Apostles Peter and Paul, and to all the Saints, that I have sinned exceedingly in thought, word and deed, through my fault, through my fault, through my most grievous fault. Therefore I beseech blessed Mary, ever Virgin, blessed Michael the Archangel, all the Saints, to pray to the Lord our God for me.

May the Almighty God have mercy on me, and forgive me my sins, and bring me to everlasting life. Amen.

May the Almighty and merciful Lord grant me pardon, absolution, and remission of all my sins. Amen.

An Act of Faith

O my God! I firmly believe that Thou art one God in three Divine persons, Father, Son and Holy Ghost; I believe that Thy Divine Son became man, and died for our sins, and that He will come to judge the living and the dead. I believe these and all the truths which the Holy Catholic Church teaches, because Thou has revealed them, who canst neither deceive nor be deceived.

An Act of Hope

O my God! Relying on Thy infinite goodness and promises, I hope to obtain pardon of my sins, the help of Thy grace, and life everlasting, through the merits of Jesus Christ, my Lord and Redeemer.

An Act of Love

O my God! I love Thee above all things, with my whole heart and soul, because Thou art all-good and worthy of all love. I love my neighbor as myself for the love of Thee. I forgive all who have injured me, and ask pardon of all whom I have injured.

An Act of Contrition

O my God! I am heartily sorry for having offended Thee, and I detest all my sins, because I dread the loss of heaven and the pains of hell, but most of all because they offend Thee, my God, who art all good and deserving of all my love. I firmly resolve, with the help of Thy grace, to confess my sins, to do penance, and to amend my life.

SHORT ACTS

Act of Faith

O my God! I believe in You and all that the Catholic Church teaches. You have told the Church what to teach us and You are all Truth. Amen.

Act of Hope

O my God! I know that You will help me to be good and help me to get to heaven, for this is what You promised to do for us. Amen.

Act of Love

O my God! I love you dearly because You are all-good. I love everybody because You love them. I want to love You forever. Amen.

Act of Contrition

O my God! I am very sorry that I have sinned against You because You are so good, and I will sin no more. Amen.

Blessing Before Meals

Bless us, O Lord, and these Thy gifts which we are about to receive from Thy bounty, through Christ our Lord. Amen.

Grace After Meals

We give Thee thanks for all Thy benefits, O Almighty God, who livest and reignest forever; and may the souls of the faithful departed, through the mercy of God, rest in peace. Amen.

Lesson 1
GOD

1. Q— Who made you?
   A— God made me.

2. Q— Who made all the people in the world?
   A— God made all the people in the world.

3. Q— What else did God make?
   A— God made all the things in the world.

4. Q— From what did God make all things?
   A— God made all things from nothing.

5. Q— To what likeness did God make us?

A— God made us to His own likeness.

6. Q— What part of us is most like to God?

A— Our soul is most like to God.

7. Q— What is the soul?

A— The soul is a spirit that will never die.

8. Q— What can God do?

A— God can do all things.

9. Q— Is anything hard for God to do?

A— Nothing is hard for God to do.

10. Q— Does God see us?

A— God does see us.

11. Q— Does God know all that we do?

A— God does know all that we do.

12. Q— Does God hear all that we say?

A— God does hear all that we say.

13. Q— Does God know what we think?

A— God does know what we think.

14. Q— How much does God know?

A— God knows all things.

Lesson 2
THE BLESSED TRINITY

1. Q— How many Gods are there?
   A— There is but one God.

2. Q— How many persons are there in God?
   A— There are three persons in God.

3. Q— What kind of persons are they?
   A— They are divine persons.

4. Q— Are these three divine persons equal in all things?
   A— These three divine persons are equal in all things.

5. Q— Name the three divine persons.

A— God the Father, God the Son, God the Holy Ghost.

6. Q— Are these three divine persons one and the same God?

A— These three divine persons are one and the same God.

7. Q— What do we call these three persons all together?

A— We call these three persons all together the Blessed Trinity.

Lesson 3
GOD- HEAVEN

1. Q- Why did God make us?

   A- God made us to be happy with Him forever in Heaven.

2. Q- Why do we live on earth?

   A- We live on earth to know God and to love Him and serve Him.

3. Q- When do we honor God?

   A- We honor God when we believe in Him, hope in Him and love Him.

4. Q- What must we believe of God?

   A- We must believe all that God has made known to the world.

5. Q— How do we know what God has made known?

A— The Catholic Church tells us what God has made known.

6. Q— What do we hope of God?

A— We hope that God will help us to be good and make us happy forever in Heaven.

7. Q— Must we love God much?

A— We must love God above all things.

8. Q— When do we serve God?

A— We serve God when we do what God wants us to do.

9. Q— How do we know what God wants us to do?
A— The Catholic Church tells us what God wants us to do.

Lesson 4
HEAVEN -- HELL

1. Q— Where do good people go when they die?

   A— Good people go to Heaven when they die.

2. Q— How long do people live in Heaven?

   A— People live forever in Heaven.

3. Q— Is everybody in Heaven happy?

   A— Everybody in Heaven is happy.

4. Q— What will we have in Heaven?

   A— We will have God and everything good in Heaven.

5. Q— Where do bad people go when they die?

A— Bad people go to Hell when they die.

6. Q— What kind of place is Hell?

A— Hell is a bad place full of fire.

7. Q— How long do bad people have to stay in Hell?

A— Bad people have to stay in Hell forever.

8. Q— Will we ever see God?

A— We will see God when we go to Heaven.

Lesson 5
THE ANGELS

1. Q— Are there angels in Heaven?
   A— There are angels in Heaven.
2. Q— What are angels?
   A— Angels are pure sprits.
3. Q— Have angels bodies?
   A— Angels have not bodies.
4. Q— Are there any angels on earth?
   A— There are angels on earth that watch over us.

5. Q— What angel watches over us?

A— Our guardian angel watches over us.

6. Q— Why does our guardian angel watch over us?

A— Our guardian angel watches over us to help us to be good.

Lesson 6
THE SIGN OF THE CROSS

1. Q— What do we say when we bless ourselves?

   A— We say: In the name of the Father, and of the Son, and of the Holy Ghost. Amen.

2. Q— Why do we say in the name of the Father, and of the Son, and of the Holy Ghost?

   A— We say in the name of the Father, and of the Son, and of the Holy Ghost to show our faith in the Blessed Trinity.

3. Q— Why do we make the Sign of the Cross?

A— We make the Sign of the Cross to show that we are Christians.

4. Q— Why is the Cross the sign of our Faith?

A— The Cross is the sign of our Faith because Christ died on it.

5. Q— What is the crucifix?

A— The crucifix is the Cross with the figure of Christ on it.

6. Q— Do we pray to the crucifix?

A— We do not pray to the crucifix.

7. Q— Do we pray before the crucifix?

A— We do pray before the crucifix.

8. Q— Of what does the crucifix remind us?

A— The crucifix reminds us that Christ died on the Cross for us.

Lesson 7
SIN

1. Q— What is sin?
   A— Anything against the law of God is a sin.

2. Q— Is it a sin to say bad words?
   A— It is a sin to say bad words.

3. Q— Is it a sin to think bad thoughts?
   A— It is a sin to think bad thoughts.

4. Q— Is it a sin to do bad things?
   A— It is a sin to do bad things.

5. Q— What is a grave sin called?
   A— A grave sin is called Mortal Sin.

6. Q— What is a slight sin called?
A— A slight sin is called a Venial Sin.

Lesson 8
ORIGINAL SIN

1. Q— Who was the first man?
A— Adam was the first man.

2. Q— Who was the first woman?
A— Eve was the first woman.

3. Q— Did Adam and Eve fall into sin?
A— Adam and Eve did fall into sin.

4. Q— What did Adam and Eve do?
A— Adam and Eve ate of the fruit that God told them not to eat.

5. Q— Does the sin of Adam and Eve come down to us?

A— The sin of Adam and Eve does come down to us.

6. Q— Are we born with sin on our soul?

A— We are born with the sin of Adam and Eve on our soul.

7. Q— What do you call the sin that comes down from Adam and Eve?

A— The sin that comes down from Adam and Eve is called Original Sin.

8. Q— Who was always free from Original Sin?

A— The Blessed Virgin Mary was always free from Original Sin.

9. Q—What is this favor to the Blessed Virgin called?

A—This favor to the Blessed Virgin Mary is called her Immaculate Conception.

Lesson 9
JESUS CHRIST

1. Q— Who came to free us from sin?

   A— Jesus Christ came to free us from sin.

2. Q— What else do we call Jesus Christ?

   A— We call Jesus Christ our Lord, our Saviour and our Redeemer.

3. Q— Is our Lord really God?

   A— Our Lord is really God.

4. Q— Is our Lord man too?

   A— Our Lord is man too.

5. Q— Where was our Lord born?
A— Our Lord was born in Bethlehem.

6. Q— Who was our Lord's mother?
A— The Blessed Virgin Mary is our Lord's mother.

7. Q— What does the Blessed Virgin Mary do for us?
A— The Blessed Virgin Mary prays to God for us.

Lesson 10
OUR LORD, OUR SAVIOUR
OUR REDEEMER

1. Q— How long did our Lord live on earth?

   A— Our Lord lived thirty-three years on earth.

2. Q— How did our Lord die?

   A— Our Lord was nailed to the Cross and died on it.

3. Q— Why did our Lord die?

   A— Our Lord died for our sins.

4. Q— On what day did our Lord die?

   A— Our Lord died on Good Friday.

5. Q— Where did our Lord die?
A— Our Lord died on Mount Calvary.

6. Q— What happened three days after our Lord died?
A— Our Lord came back to life three days after He died.

Lesson 11
THE RESURRECTION
THE ASCENSION

1. Q— On what day did our Lord come back to life?

   A— Our Lord came back to life on Easter Sunday.

2. Q— What does the Resurrection mean?

   A— The Resurrection means that our Lord came back to life.

3. Q— How long did our Lord stay on earth after He arose from the dead?

   A— Our Lord stayed forty days on earth after he arose from the dead.

4. Q— Where did our Lord go after forty days?

A— After forty days, our Lord went up to Heaven.

5. Q— What do you call the day on which our Lord went up to Heaven?

A— The day on which our Lord went up to Heaven is called Ascension Day.

Lesson 12
THE CHURCH

1. Q— Whom did our Lord send after He went up to Heaven?

   A— Our Lord sent the Holy Ghost to earth after He went up to Heaven.

2. Q— Why did our Lord send the Holy Ghost to earth?

   A— Our Lord sent the Holy Ghost to stay with His Church.

3. Q— What does the Holy Ghost do for the Church?

   A— The Holy Ghost guides the Church in all truth.

4. Q— Which is Christ's Church?
A— The Catholic Church is Christ's Church.

5. Q— Who founded the Catholic Church?
A— Christ founded the Catholic Church.

6. Q— Who founded the other churches?
A— Men founded the other churches.

7. Q— What do we call the teachings of the Catholic Church?
A— We call the teachings of the Catholic Church our Faith.

8. Q— Who is the head of the Catholic Church?

A— Christ is the head of the Catholic Church.

9. Q— What is the pope?

A— The pope is the head bishop of the world.

10. Q— What does the pope do?

A— The pope rules the Church for our Lord.

11. Q— Who was the first pope?

A— Saint Peter was the first pope.

12. Q— Can the Catholic Church teach anything false?

A— The Catholic Church can not teach anything false.

13. Q— Why can not the Catholic Church teach anything false?

A— The Catholic Church can not teach anything false because the Holy Ghost guides it.

14. Q— How long will the Catholic Church last?

A— The Catholic Church will last until the end of the world.

Lesson 13
THE LAST JUDGEMENT

1. Q— Will our Lord come back to the earth again?

   A— Our Lord will come back to the earth again on the last day of the world.

2. Q— Why will our Lord come on the last day?

   A— Our Lord will come to judge us on the last day.

3. Q— Will our Lord judge the people that are dead?

   A— Our Lord will judge the people that are dead.

4. Q— How will our Lord judge the dead people?

A— Our Lord will bring the dead people back to life to judge them.

5. Q— Why will our Lord judge us?

A— Our Lord will judge us to show whether we are good or bad.

6. Q— What is the last day of the world called?

A— The last day of the world is called the Judgment Day.

7. Q— What is the last Judgment called?

A— The last judgement is called the General Judgment.

Lesson 14
THE PARTICULAR JUDGMENT.
PURGATORY.

1. Q— Will our Lord judge us any other time?

   A— Our Lord will judge each one of us when we die.

2. Q— What is the Judgment after death called?

   A— The Judgment after death is called the Particular Judgment.

3. Q— Where do people go that die with Venial sins on their souls?

   A— People that die with Venial sins on their souls go to Purgatory.

4. Q— Who else go to Purgatory?

A— Those who have not done enough penance for their sins go to Purgatory.

5. Q— Can we help the souls in Purgatory?

A— We can help the souls in Purgatory by praying for them.

6. Q— What do our prayers do for the souls in Purgatory?

A— Our prayers help to free the souls from Purgatory.

7. Q— Where do souls go when they leave Purgatory?

A— Souls go to Heaven when they leave Purgatory.

8. Q— Will there always be a Purgatory?

A— There will be no Purgatory after the end of the world.

Lesson 15
DIVINE GRACE. THE SACRAMENTS

1. Q— How can we save our soul?

   A— We can save our soul through God's grace.

2. Q— Can we go to Heaven without God's grace?

   A— We can not go to Heaven without God's grace.

3. Q— What does God's grace do for us?

   A— God's grace makes us holy and helps us to do good.

4. Q— How does God's grace come to us?

A— God's grace comes to us through prayer and the Sacraments.

5. Q— How many Sacraments are there?

A— There are seven Sacraments.

6. Q— Who gave us the Sacraments?

A— Our Lord gave us the Sacraments.

Lesson 16
BAPTISM

1. Q— What is the first Sacrament?

   A— Baptism is the first Sacrament.

2. Q— What does Baptism do for us?

   A— Baptism takes away Original Sin.

3. Q— Do we have to be baptized?

   A— We do have to be baptized.

4. Q— Why do we have to be baptized?

   A— We can not go to Heaven if we are not baptized.

5. Q— Who baptizes us?

A— The priest baptizes us.

Lesson 17
CONFIRMATION

1. Q— What Sacrament makes us strong in the faith?

   A— Confirmation is the Sacrament that makes us strong in faith.

2. Q— What do we receive in Confirmation?

   A— We receive the Holy Ghost in Confirmation.

3. Q— Why do we receive the Holy Ghost?

   A— We receive the Holy Ghost to make us good and strong Christians.

4. Q— Who gives us Confirmation?

   A— The Bishop gives Confirmation.

Lesson 18
THE HOLY EUCHARIST

1. Q— What is the Sacrament of our Lord's body and blood?

   A— The Holy Eucharist is the Sacrament of our Lord's body and blood.

2. Q— What does the Holy Eucharist contain?

   A— The Holy Eucharist contains our Lord's body and blood.

3. Q— Does the Holy Eucharist also contain our Lord's Soul and Divinity?

   A— The Holy Eucharist does contain our Lord's Soul and Divinity.

4. Q— Under what form is our Lord present in the Holy Eucharist?

A— Our Lord is present under the form of bread and wine.

5. Q— Who changes bread and wine into our Lord's body and blood?

A— The priest changes bread and wine into our Lord's body and blood.

6. Q— Who gave the priest power to change bread and wine into our Lord's body and blood?

A— Our Lord Himself gave the priest power to change bread and wine into His body and blood.

7. Q— When do we receive the Holy Eucharist?

A— We receive the Holy Eucharist when we go to Holy Communion.

8. Q— How often should we go to Holy Communion?

A— We should go to Holy Communion every day if we can.

9. Q— Must we be free from sin when we go to Holy Communion?

A— We must be free from mortal sin when we go to Holy Communion.

10. Q— What must we do before Holy Communion if we are in mortal sin?

A— If we are in mortal sin, we must go to confession before Holy Communion.

11. Q— Are we allowed to eat or drink anything before Holy Communion?

A— We are not allowed to eat or drink anything from the midnight before we go to Holy Communion.

12. Q— What must we do after Holy Communion?

A— After Holy Communion we must stay awhile and pray to God to thank Him.

Lesson 19
THE MASS

1. Q— When does the priest change bread and wine into our Lord's body and blood?

   A— The priest changes bread and wine into our Lord's body and blood when he says Mass.

2. Q— What is the Mass?

   A— The Mass is the sacrifice of our Lord's body and blood.

3. Q— When did our Lord sacrifice His body and blood in another way?

   A— Our Lord sacrificed His body and blood on the Cross.

4. Q— In what way is the Mass like our Lord's death on the Cross?

A— The Mass and our Lord's death on the Cross are one and the same sacrifice.

5. Q— How often must we go to Mass?

A— We must go to Mass every Sunday and Holy Day.

6. Q— Is it a sin to miss Mass on Sundays and Holy Days?

A— It is a mortal sin wilfully to miss Mass on Sundays and Holy Days.

7. Q— Should we go to Mass on other days too?

A— It is good to go to Mass every day if we can.

Lesson 20
THE SACRAMENT OF PENANCE.

1. Q— What Sacrament takes away our sins?

   A— The Sacrament of Penance takes away our sins.

2. Q— What sins does the Sacrament of Penance take away?

   A— The Sacrament of Penance takes away the sins we fall into after Baptism.

3. Q— Who takes away our sins in the Sacrament of Penance?

   A— The priest takes away our sins in the Sacrament of Penance.

4. Q— Who gave the priest the power to take away our sins?

A— Our Lord gave the priest the power to take way our sins.

5. Q— What must we do to have our sins taken way.

A— We must go to Confession to have our sins taken away.

Lesson 21
CONFESSION

1. Q— What must we do in Confession?

   A— We must tell our sins to the priest in Confession.

2. Q— What else is necessary in Confession?

   A— We must be sorry for our sins in Confession.

3. Q— Can we be forgiven if we are not sorry for our sins?

   A— We can not be forgiven if we are not sorry for our sins.

4. Q— What must we promise in Confession?

A— We must promise to try never to fall into sin any more.

5. Q— What does the priest give us to do after Confession?

A— The priest gives us a penance to do after Confession.

6. Q— What is a penance?

A— A penance is some prayers or good works to atone for our sins.

Lesson 22
EXTREME UNCTION.
HOLY ORDERS. MATRIMONY.

1. Q— What Sacrament do we receive when we are going to die?

A— We receive the Sacrament of Extreme Unction when we are going to die.

2. Q— How does the priest give Extreme Unction?

A— The priest anoints the sick person with holy oil when he gives Extreme Unction.

3. Q— In what Sacrament are priests ordained?

A— Priest are ordained in the Sacrament of Holy Orders.

4. Q— Who gives Holy Orders?

A— The Bishop gives Holy Orders.

5. Q— In what Sacrament do people get married?

A— People get married in the Sacrament of Matrimony.

6. Q— Who can marry Catholics?

A— The priest alone can marry Catholics.

7. Q— Are Catholics really married if they go to anybody else than the priest to get married?

A— Catholics are not really married if they go to anybody else than the priest to get married.

8. Q— What are the seven Sacraments?

A— The seven Sacraments are: Baptism, Confirmation, Holy Eucharist, Penance, Extreme Unction, Holy Orders, and Matrimony.

Lesson 23
THE FIRST COMMANDMENT

1. Q— What is the First Commandment?

A— I am the Lord thy God, thou shalt not have strange gods before me.

2. Q— What does the First Commandment tell us to do?

A— The first Commandment tells us to adore God alone.

3. Q— Does the First Commandment tell us to study our Catechism?

A— The First Commandment does tell us to study our Catechism.

4. Q— Why do we study Catechism?

A— We study Catechism to learn all about our faith.

5. Q— Is it a sin to be ashamed of your Faith?

A— It is a sin to be ashamed of your Faith.

6. Q— Is it a sin to believe in fortune-tellers?

A— It is a sin to believe in fortune tellers.

7. Q— It it a sin to believe in charms, dreams and such things?

A— It is a sin to believe in charms, dreams and such things.

Lesson 24
PRAYER

1. Q— Does the First Commandment tell us to say our prayers?

   A— The First Commandment does tell us to say our prayers.

2. Q— What does it mean to say our prayers?

   A— To say our prayers means to talk with God.

3. Q— Why do we pray to God?

   A— We pray to God to ask for His graces and blessings.

4. Q— How often should we say our prayers?

A— We should say our prayers every morning and night.

5. Q— What other times should we pray?

A— We should pray during Mass, before and after meals and whenever we need God's help.

6. Q— How should we pray?

A— We should try to think of what we are saying when we pray.

7. Q— Do we pray to anybody else than God?

A— We pray to the Blessed Virgin and the saints.

8. Q— Why do we pray to the Blessed Virgin and the saints?

A— We pray to the Blessed Virgin and the saints to ask them to help us with God.

9. Q— Why do we have crosses, statues and holy pictures?

A— We have crosses, statues and holy pictures to put us in mind of God and the saints.

Lesson 25
THE SECOND COMMANDMENT

1. Q— What is the Second Commandment?

   A— Thou shalt not take the name of the Lord thy God in vain.

2. Q— What does the Second Commandment tell us to do?

   A— The Second Commandment tells us to respect God's name.

3. Q— What name should we honor most?

   A— We should honor most the Holy name of Jesus.

4. Q— Is it a sin to curse and swear?

A— It is a sin to curse and swear.

5. Q— What is an oath?

A— An oath is to call on God to see that we tell the truth.

6. Q— Is it a sin to take a false oath?

A— It is a mortal sin to take a false oath.

7. Q— What is a vow?

A— A vow is a solemn promise to God to do something good.

Lesson 26

THE THIRD COMMANDMENT

1. Q— What is the Third Commandment?

   A— Remember thou keep holy the Lord's day.

2. Q— What does the Third Commandment tell us to do?

   A— The Third Commandment tells us to go to Mass on Sundays and Holy Days.

3. Q— Should we go to church at other times too?

   A— We should always try to go to church when there are Vespers or other Devotions.

4. Q— Is it a sin to work on Sundays and Holy Days?

A— It is a sin to work on Sundays and Holy Days unless we have to work.

5. Q— Is it a sin to play on Sunday?

A— It is not a sin to play on Sunday if we do not miss Mass.

6. Q— Is it wrong to sew and bake and wash and iron on Sunday?

A— It is wrong to sew and bake and wash and iron on Sunday.

7. Q— Is it wrong to cook and sweep on Sunday?

A— It is not wrong to cook and sweep on Sunday.

Lesson 27
THE FOURTH COMMANDMENT

1. Q— What is the Fourth Commandment?

   A— Honor thy father and thy mother.

2. Q— What does the Fourth Commandment tell us to do?

   A— The Fourth Commandment tells us to obey our father and mother.

3. Q— Must we be kind to our parents?

   A— We must be kind to our parents and love them.

4. Q— Is it wrong to talk back to our parents?

A— It is wrong to talk back to our parents.

5. Q— Should we help our parents?

A— We should help our parents in every way we can.

6. Q— Must we obey anybody else?

A— We must also obey our pastors and our teachers.

7. Q— Must we also obey the law of the land?

A— We must also obey the law of the land.

Lesson 28
THE FIFTH COMMANDMENT

1. Q— What is the Fifth Commandment?
A— Thou shalt not kill.

2. Q— What is the worst sin against the Fifth Commandment?
A— The worst sin against the Fifth Commandment is murder.

3. Q— Is it a sin to get angry?
A— It is a sin to get angry.

4. Q— Is it a sin to fight and quarrel?
A— It is a sin to fight and quarrel.

5. Q— Is it a sin to get drunk?

A— It is a sin to get drunk.

Lesson 29
THE SIXTH COMMANDMENT

1. Q— What is the Sixth Commandment?

   A— Thou shalt not commit adultery.

2. Q— What does the Sixth Commandment tell us to do?

   A— The Sixth Commandment tells us to be pure at all times.

3. Q— When are we pure?

   A— We are pure when we keep from all bad thoughts, words and actions.

4. Q— Is it a sin to look at bad things?

   A— It is a sin to look at bad things.

5. Q— Is it a sin to look at bad pictures?

A— It is a sin to look at bad pictures.

6. Q— Is it a sin to read bad things?

A— It is a sin to read bad things.

7. Q— Is it a sin to read bad books and papers?

A— It is a sin to read bad books and papers.

8. Q— Is it a sin to play with bad things?

A— It is a sin to play with bad things.

Lesson 30
THE SEVENTH COMMANDMENT

1. Q— What is the Seventh Commandment?

   A— Thou shalt not steal.

2. Q— What does the Seventh Commandment tell us?

   A— The Seventh Commandment tells us never to take what belongs to somebody else.

3. Q— What must people do that steal?

   A— People that steal must pay back what they steal.

4. Q— Why must they pay back what they steal?

A— They can not be forgiven if they are not willing to pay back what they steal.

5. Q— Is it a sin to break other people's things?

A— It is a sin to break other people's things on purpose.

6. Q— Is it a sin to spoil other people's things?

A— It is a sin to spoil other people's things on purpose.

7. Q— What must we do if we break and spoil other people's things?

A— If we break or spoil other people's things we must pay for them.

Lesson 31
THE EIGHTH COMMANDMENT

1. Q— What is the Eighth Commandment?

    A— Thou shalt not bear false witness against thy neighbor.

2. Q— What does the Eighth Commandment tell us?

    A— The Eighth Commandment tells us never to lie.

3. Q— When should we tell the truth?

    A— We should tell the truth at all times.

4. Q— Should we ever be afraid to tell the truth?

A— We should never be afraid to tell the truth.

5. Q— Is it a sin to tell a lie?

A— It is a sin to tell a lie.

6. Q— Is it a sin to tell bad things about others?

A— It is a sin to tell bad things about others.

7. Q— What must they do who tell bad things about others?

A— They who tell bad things about others must go and make up for the harm they have done.

8. Q— What should you do before Confession if you are angry and do not speak with somebody?

A— If you are angry and do not speak, you should go and make up before you go to Confession.

Lesson 32
THE NINTH AND TENTH COMMANDMENTS

1. Q— What is the Ninth Commandment?

   A— Thou shalt not covet thy neighbor's wife.

2. Q— What is the Tenth Commandment?

   A— Thou shalt not covet thy neighbor's goods.

3. Q— What does the Tenth Commandment tell us?

   A— The Tenth Commandment tells us not to wish for what belongs to somebody else.

4. Q— Does the Tenth Commandment tell us not to envy anybody?

A— The Tenth Commandment does tell us not to envy anybody.

Lesson 33
THE TEN COMMANDMENTS

Q. Name the Ten Commandments

A.

1. I am the Lord thy God, thou shalt not have strange gods before me.

2. Thou shalt not take the name of the Lord thy God in vain.

3. Remember thou keep holy the Lord's day.

4. Honor thy father and thy mother.

5. Thou shalt not kill.

6. Thou shalt not commit adultery.

7. Thou shalt not steal.

8. Thou shalt not bear false witness against thy neighbor.

9. Thou shalt not covet thy neighbor's wife.

10. Thou shalt not covet thy neighbor's goods.

Lesson 34
THE COMMANDMENTS OF THE CHURCH

Q— What are the chief Commandments of the Church?

A— The chief Commandments of the Church are these six:

1. To hear Mass on Sundays and Holy Days of obligation.

2. To fast and abstain on the days appointed.

3. To confess our sins at least once a year.

4. To receive the Holy Eucharist during the Easter time.

5. To contribute to the support of our pastors and to the maintenance of the church and school.

6. Not to into into the marriage contract except before the priest and two witnesses, nor to marry non-Catholics nor those who are related to us within the third degree of kindred, nor to solemnize marriage at forbidden times.

Made in the USA
Las Vegas, NV
19 July 2024

92609065R00057